FANGBONE!
THIRD-GRADE BARBARIAN

MICHAEL REX

SCHOLASTIC INC.
New York Toronto London Auckland
Sydney Mexico City New Delhi Hong Kong

ISBN 978-0-545-44042-4

12 11 10 9 8 7 6 5 4 3 2 1   12 13 14 15 16 17/0

Printed in the U.S.A.   23

This edition first printing, April 2012

Design by Ryan Thomann
Text set in CC Wild Words
The art was created in ink and colored digitally.

TO MIKE CHEN,
FOR MAKING ME A STORYTELLER
INSTEAD OF A DOODLER

IN A WORLD OF SWORDS, MAGIC, BARBARIANS, AND EVIL BIG TOES...

PICK YOUR OWN ARMPITS, YOU SWAMP-WATER GREASE-FISH!

WATCH YOUR MOUTH, BOY! YOUR JOB IN THIS CLAN IS TO SERVE THE WARRIORS!

I **AM** A WARRIOR!

HA! A WARRIOR? YOU'RE JUST A RUNT!

YOU ARE LOWER TO THE GROUND THAN A PUS-FILLED PIMPLE ON THE BELLY OF A SLOP-HOG!

AND MORE USELESS THAN A SWORD MADE OF DONKEY DUNG!

I AM USEFUL! AND I CAN FIGHT! ONE DAY I'LL HAVE MY OWN ARMY!

HA! HA! HA! HA! HA! HA! HA! HA! HA! HA!

RIGHT, AN ARMY OF SCRUBBY LITTLE SNOT-NOSED MITES LIKE YOURSELF?

OOOH! I CAN HEAR THE ENEMY SHAKING IN THEIR ARMOR!

9

KEEP THE TOE FROM DROOL...HURRY...
IF DROOL GETS HIS TOE,
THE CLANS WILL BE DESTROYED...
HURRY...DROOL'S ARMY IS CLOSE...
VERY CLOSE...

HMMMM...

GRIMEBLADE, YOU WILL GO!

I CANNOT GO! I AM THE BEST SWORDSMAN HERE. YOU NEED ME TO FIGHT!

CLAPPERCLAW, YOU TAKE THE TOE AND GO!

I CANNOT GO! I AM THE BEST AXE SWINGER HERE!

GIZZARDFOOT, YOU GO!

HURRY!

I CANNOT GO! I AM THE... SMELLIEST ONE HERE!

AXEBEAR! THE ARMY OF DROOL!

AAAAAAAAAHH!

I AM CERTAINLY NOT RUNNING AWAY AND MISSING THE BATTLE!

WHO WILL GO?

SEND ME!

14

PROTECT IT! NEVER LET IT GO!

DO NOT FEAR! I WILL FIND AN ARMY TO FIGHT WITH OUR CLAN!

NO! NO ARMY! DO AS YOU ARE TOLD! BLEND IN. DO NOT ATTRACT ATTENTION!

MAY THE LUCK OF BIGBELLY BLACKSPIT FOLLOW YOU!

NOW GO, BOY! **GO!**

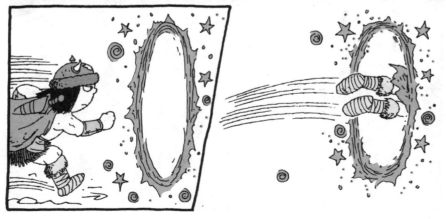

VOOOP!

BONK!

BEAST! GET BACK!

GET BACK, I SAY!

TOWN DUMP

22

IN CLASS 3G...

MS. GILLIAN, THIS IS FANGBONE. HE'S NEW IN OUR CLASS.

HUH? NO ONE TOLD ME ABOUT A NEW STUDENT.

MAYBE YOU'RE IN THE WRONG CLASS.

HERE, MAKE A NAME TAG FOR NOW.

FANGBONE, CAN YOU WRITE YOUR NAME?

NO.

CAN YOU READ?

NO.

OK...OK... YOU'RE IN THE RIGHT CLASS. WELCOME TO 3G. EVERYONE HERE LEARNS AT THEIR OWN SPEED.

BOYS AND GIRLS? WE HAVE A NEW STUDENT IN CLASS. SAY HI TO FANGBONE.

Hi! Hi!

Hi! YO!

IS FANGBONE YOUR FIRST OR LAST NAME?

I AM FANGBONE THE YOUNG, OF THE MIGHTY LIZARD CLAN.

SON OF STEELBEARD THE BOLD, GRANDSON TO LOCKJAW THE FEARLESS.

GREAT-GRANDSON OF WEASEL-EYE THE SLIPPERY!

25

WHY DO YOU HAVE A SWORD?

I AM A WARRIOR! I USE IT TO FIGHT THE ARMY OF DROOL!

WHY DO YOU WEAR THAT HELMET?

TO PROTECT MY SKULL IN BATTLE!

WHY IS YOUR UNDERWEAR MADE OUT OF FUR?

FUR UNDERWEAR IS STUPID.

IT KEEPS ME WARM IN THE FROZEN WINTERS OF SKULLBANIA!

IS SKULLBANIA IN NEW JERSEY?

WHY IS YOUR HAIR SO LONG?

WHAT ARE THOSE THINGS ON YOUR ARMS?

WHY ARE YOUR BOOTS ALL RAGGY?

DO YOU LIKE GLITTER?

CLASS? CLASS! PLEASE RELAX. FANGBONE COMES FROM A FARAWAY PLACE. PEOPLE ARE DIFFERENT ALL OVER THE WORLD. WE MUST RESPECT HIS CULTURE.

BEEP! BEEP! BEEP!

DIBBY, YOU ARE NOT A ROBOT. ASK YOUR QUESTION IN ENGLISH.

WHY DID YOU COME TO OUR SCHOOL?

I AM HERE TO PROTECT THE BIG TOE OF DROOL!

WHAT'S THE BIG TOE OF DROOL?

FIVE HUNDRED WINTERS AGO,
THE GREATEST EVIL THAT EVER LIVED RULED OVER
SKULLBANIA. VENOMOUS DROOL WAS HIS NAME.
HE BUILT AN ARMY THAT SWEPT THROUGH THE LANDS
AND ALMOST WIPED OUT THE CLANS.

MANY BATTLES WERE FOUGHT, AND MANY GREAT
WARRIORS DIED TO KEEP HIS EVIL FROM SPREADING.

FINALLY, DROOL
WAS DEFEATED, AND CUT
INTO MANY SMALL PIECES...

WHOA! FANGBONE, THIS MIGHT NOT BE APPROPRIATE FOR OUR CLASSROOM.

MORE! MORE!!!

THE PIECES WERE SEPARATED AND TAKEN TO DIFFERENT LANDS
SO THAT VENOMOUS DROOL COULD NEVER RULE AGAIN.

BUT SINCE MY BIRTH, A NEW ARMY OF DROOL WORSHIPERS
HAS BEEN MOVING THROUGH SKULLBANIA, COLLECTING
THE PIECES ONE BY ONE, AND REBUILDING DROOL.

THE ONLY PIECE THAT THEY DO NOT HAVE IS HIS BIG TOE!
MY CLAN WAS PUT IN CHARGE OF PROTECTING THE BIG TOE
BECAUSE IT IS THE MOST EVIL, CURSED, WRETCHED
PART OF HIS BODY.

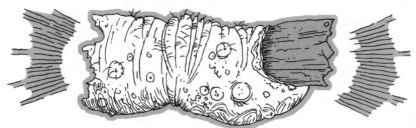

YES. YOU HAVE TO PLAY. C'MON, IT CAN'T BE THAT BAD.

YOU NEVER GOT BEANED BY DUNCAN MCDUFF.

WINNING IS IMPOSSIBLE.

NOTHING IS IMPOSSIBLE WITH TEAMWORK.

WHAT IF THE WHOLE TEAM STINKS?

CAN WE AT LEAST CHANGE THE NAME OF THE TEAM?

SORRY, WE ALREADY MADE POSTERS AND T-SHIRTS.

BUT EVERYONE LAUGHS AT "EXTREME ATTACK UNICORNS."

EXTREME ATTACK UNICORNS

HEH.

A LITTLE LATER...

BILL, I HAVE TO MAKE.

MAKE WHAT?

MAKE... DROPPINGS.

OH! YOU GOTTA POOP.

MS. GILLIAN, CAN I SHOW FANGBONE THE BOYS' ROOM?

YES.

SEE?

HERE'S THE SINK...

BY THE GODS OF SKULLBANIA! THIS IS SORCERY!!

NOPE.

IT'S PLUMBING.

AFTER LUNCH...

HEY, KID, WHAT'S WITH THE SWORD?

LEAVE HIM ALONE, DUNCAN.

I DON'T EAT MY BOOGERS!

NO. YOU EAT SWORDBOY'S BOOGERS!

SHUT UP!

HA. ANOTHER FREAK FOR 3G!

THANKS FOR STOPPING ME. I'LL BE SUSPENDED IF I GET INTO ANOTHER FIGHT.

DON'T TALK TO DUNCAN. HE'S THE MEANEST JERK IN THE WHOLE THIRD GRADE.

BILL, WHAT IS A BOOGER-EATER?

DUH. A KID THAT EATS BOOGERS!

BOOGERS? WHAT IS BOOGERS?

Y'KNOW, THE JUNK THAT COMES OUT OF YOUR NOSE.

AH...MY CLAN CALLS THAT "GLOOBUS." THERE WAS ONCE A GREAT WARRIOR LOST IN THE DESERT OF HORRIBLE PAIN FOR TWO WINTERS.

HE SURVIVED BY EATING ONLY HIS GLOOBUS.

AND THE GLOOBUS OF HIS CAMEL.
HE WAS FOREVER AFTER CALLED "GLOOBUS THE GREAT."

BALL! HEADS UP!

WHOOOOOO

YOU HAVE TO PLAY. YOU'RE IN 3G, AND 3G PLAYS ON FRIDAY.

NO. I NEED ONLY TO PROTECT THE BIG TOE OF DROOL!

...AND BUILD AN ARMY.

AFTER SCHOOL...

BILL, I NEED SOMEWHERE TO SLEEP TONIGHT. DO YOU KNOW OF ANY INNS?

UM... VACATION INN IS OUT ON THE HIGHWAY, BUT YOU NEED A CREDIT CARD.

WHAT ABOUT A SHELTER, OR A CAVE?

YEAH! I KNOW A CAVE!

IT'S IN THE WOODS NEAR MY HOUSE. C'MON!

PIK! POK! POKE!

43

45

BY THE AXE OF GLOR, ATTACK US!

FWIP! FWOP! FWOOP!

HA! THE WATER HAS TURNED THEM TO MUD! BILL, YOU ARE A CUNNING WARRIOR!

THANKS. IT WAS JUST TEAMWORK.

AH! TEAMWORK. IT IS THE WAY OF THE WARRIOR. YOU WATCH MY BACK, I WATCH YOURS.

 WHERE DID THEY COME FROM?

THEY WERE SENT FROM MY WORLD TO GET THE BIG TOE.

 DROOL KNOWS WHERE I AM.

I MUST BUILD MY ARMY QUICKLY!

BILL! YOU WILL BE MY WAR CHIEF. I SHALL CALL YOU **BILL THE BEAST!**

 SWEET.

SWEET.

POUND!

 A WHILE LATER....

HERE'S THE CAVE.

I WILL BUILD A FIRE.

 BUT WE DON'T HAVE ANY--

--MATCHES.

THIS CAVE WILL DO.

BILL THE BEAST, TODAY WAS VERY ODD FOR ME. THIS WORLD IS DIFFERENT FROM MINE. I NEED YOUR HELP.

SURE.

WHERE CAN WE FIND WARRIORS?

GEEZ...I DON'T KNOW. YOU CAN'T JUST BUY AN ARMY AT THE MALL.

THINK ABOUT IT TONIGHT. TOMORROW, WE WILL FIND AN ARMY. THE GREATEST ARMY EVER!

WE WILL CRUSH DROOL AND HIS HORDE INTO DUST THAT WILL BLOW IN THE WIND FOR ALL TIME.

YES, SIR!!

THE NEXT MORNING...

NO, I DON'T WANT TO BE IN YOUR ARMY!

BIKES REPAIR

JUST BECAUSE I'M BIG AND TOUGH-LOOKING AND HAVE TATTOOS, YOU THINK I LIKE FIGHTING? I HATE VIOLENCE! NOW, BEAT IT!

ARENA

HOCKEY PRACTICE 6:00 AM

I'M ALWAYS UP FOR A GOOD FIGHT. WHAT ARE YOU PAYING?

WE HAVE NO GOLD. YOU WILL FIGHT TO STOP EVIL AND DEFEND THE HONOR OF THE CLANS.

SORRY, BOYS, HONOR WON'T BUY ME NEW TEETH.

WE WON'T JOIN *YOUR* ARMY, BUT IF YOU WANT TO JOIN OURS, COME BACK WHEN YOU'RE 18.

NOW GET TO SCHOOL!

IN SCHOOL....

GOOD MORNING, DIBBY.

WHY ARE YOU WEARING A CAPE?

IF FANGBONE GETS TO WEAR A CAPE, I GET TO WEAR A CAPE.

GOOD MORNING, PATTY. WHAT'S WITH THE HELMET?

IF FANGBONE CAN WEAR A HELMET, I CAN WEAR A HELMET. SEE THE GLITTER?

ROBERT, WHERE IS YOUR SHIRT?

IF FANGBONE DOESN'T HAVE TO WEAR A SHIRT, NEITHER DO I!

EDDY, IS THAT FUR UNDERWEAR?

IF--

OK. OK. ENOUGH!

WHERE DO YOU EVEN GET FUR UNDERWEAR?

WOW. WHAT'S GOING ON?

THE WHOLE CLASS WANTS TO DRESS LIKE OUR NEW STUDENT FROM SKULLBANIA.

FANTASTIC! LEARNING ABOUT OTHER CULTURES THROUGH THEIR CLOTHING.

BRILLIANT. BRILLIANT! KEEP IT UP, MS. GILLIAN!

IS SKULLBANIA IN NEW JERSEY?

AFTER SCHOOL....

MOM! I'M HOME!

BILL,
YOU LIVE
LIKE A KING.

YOUR
DWELLING IS
MAGNIFICENT.

YOUR DUNGEON
MUST BE JUST
AS WICKED.

MOM? THIS IS
FANGBONE. HE'S
A NEW KID IN
SCHOOL.

HI.

GREETINGS,
MOTHER
OF BILL.

HE'S FROM
SKULLBANIA.

SKULLBANIA?
IS THAT IN
NEW JERSEY?

CAN WE HAVE
A SNACK?

WHAT'S THE
MAGIC WORD?

ZORKO!

GORKO!

DORKO!

DOO!

HUH?

ZORKO!

GORKO!

DORKO!

DOO!

THE MAGIC WORD!

ACTUALLY, THE MAGIC WORD IS "PLEASE."

PAT PAT

WHAT A MYSTERIOUS LAND THIS IS.

BILL, TAKE YOUR MEDICINE!

OK, MOM.

WHAT IS THAT FOR?

SO I DON'T GO ALL HYPER, LIKE BLAAAAAHHH.

IT HELPS ME CONCENTRATE. WANT A SNACK?

SNACK? WHAT IS SNACK?

I DON'T KNOW. SOMETHING YOU EAT WHEN YOU'RE NOT HUNGRY.

DO YOU HAVE VULTURE BEAK STEW?

NO... BUT WE HAVE... YES! HOT WINGS!!

THESE ARE MY FAVORITE. TRY THESE.

THEY'RE "ATOMIC" HOT.

THUD!

TOO MUCH, HUH?

THEY ARE WORSE THAN DEMON GLOOBUS.

I THOUGHT A WARRIOR WOULD LIKE THEM.

CLINK
BONK

HERE. THIS IS MOM'S MEAT LOAF. I THINK IT'S PRETTY GROSS, BUT YOU CAN TRY IT.

AHHHH! THIS IS THE FOOD OF THE GODS!

GREETINGS, MOTHER OF BILL.

FANGBONE SAYS YOUR MEAT LOAF IS BETTER THAN VULTURE BEAK STEW.

I GUESS THAT'S A COMPLIMENT.

WHAT ARE YOU BOYS UP TO?

WE'RE GOING TO FIND AN ARMY.

SOUNDS LIKE FUN. I'LL BE IN THE GARDEN.

MAY YOUR HARVEST BE RICH AND GENEROUS.

I LIKE YOU! YOU'RE FUNNY.

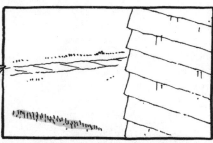

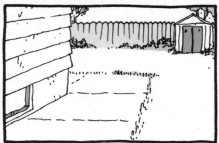

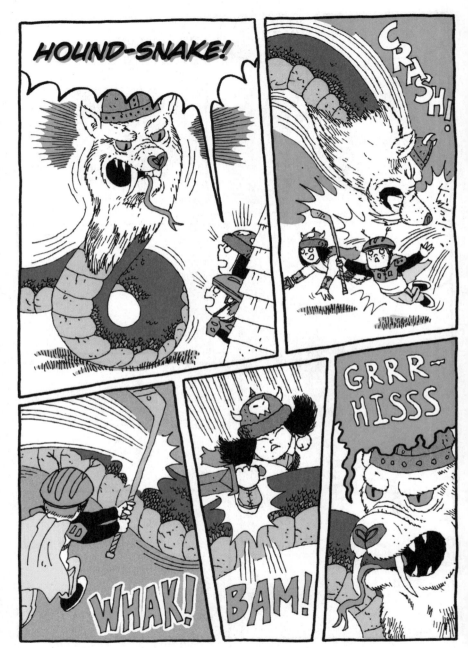

HA! NOTHING CAN STAND UP TO A WHOLE BUCKET OF ATOMIC WINGS!

BILL THE BEAST! YOU ARE MORE THAN A WAR CHIEF! YOU ARE A SORCERER AS WELL!

COOL. ARE SORCERERS SMART?

THE SMARTEST! YOU MUST BE THE MOST HONORED IN YOUR SCHOOL.

NO WAY. SCHOOL IS FOR KIDS WHO CAN SIT AT A DESK ALL DAY WITHOUT MOVING.

SIT! SIT! SIT! AND YOU HAVE TO KNOW ONLY THE ANSWERS THE TEACHER WANTS. THEY DON'T CARE IF YOU KNOW OTHER THINGS. LIKE HOW TO STOP A HOUND-SNAKE.

MAGGOT TEETH!

WARRIORS
DO NOT GET SCARED.

WARRIORS
GET UNEASY.

DUUUDE! YOUR AIM IS PERFECT. YOU GOTTA PLAY BEANBALL!

WE COULD SO TOTALLY WIN!

I TOLD YOU, BILL, WARRIORS DO NOT PLAY GAMES.

YOU MAY BE A WARRIOR, BUT YOU'RE A KID, TOO. KIDS PLAY GAMES.

I AM NOT PLAYING.

IN THE CLASSROOM...

OK, BOYS AND GIRLS... THE OTHER DAY WE WERE TALKING ABOUT THE EARTH. DOES ANYONE REMEMBER WHY IT LOOKS LIKE THE SUN "RISES" IN THE MORNING?

FANGBONE?

MANY THOUSANDS OF WINTERS AGO, THE WORLD WAS TOTALLY DARK. A BEAUTIFUL BUT EVIL PRINCESS NAMED ZIZZELLA RULED OVER THE ENTIRE LAND.

A GREAT WARRIOR NAMED STONEBACK THE SOLID ASKED ZIZZELLA TO MARRY HIM. SHE AGREED, BUT ONLY IF HE COULD BRING HER THE EYE OF THE CYCLOPTOPUS.

FOR YEARS, STONEBACK SEARCHED FOR THE FEARSOME CYCLOPTOPUS, WHICH WAS HARD TO FIND IN A WORLD THAT WAS TOTALLY DARK. FINALLY HE FOUND IT, SLAYED IT, AND RETURNED WITH THE EYE.

BUT ZIZZELLA NEVER WANTED TO MARRY STONEBACK.
SHE THOUGHT THAT THE CYCLOPTOPUS WOULD EAT HIM
AND HE WOULD NEVER RETURN. WHEN HE SHOWED UP FOR
THE WEDDING, SHE AND HER SUBJECTS WERE GONE.

STONEBACK WAS FURIOUS! HE VOWED TO FIND HER.
BUT IT WAS EASY TO HIDE IN A WORLD THAT WAS ALWAYS
DARK. IN A RAGE, STONEBACK SET THE
CYCLOPTOPUS EYE ON FIRE AND
KICKED IT INTO THE SKY.

THE EYE
LIT UP THE LAND,
AND DAY WAS CREATED.

EVERY DAY, STONEBACK THE SOLID KICKS THE BURNING EYE INTO THE SKY AND SEARCHES FOR ZIZZELLA!

THAT'S QUITE A STORY, FANGBONE.

IT IS NOT A STORY. IT IS TRUTH.

BUT IT'S NOT THE ANSWER WE WERE LOOKING FOR, FANGBONE. ACTUALLY, THE EARTH ROTATES.

ROTATES? NONSENSE.

MS. GILLIAN? YOU SAID THAT WE HAVE TO ACCEPT OTHER PEOPLE'S CULTURES AND THE THINGS THAT THEY THINK. RIGHT?

YES, BUT...

WELL, IF THAT'S WHAT FANGBONE THINKS, THAT'S WHAT I THINK!

GIANT BURNING EYES ARE MUCH COOLER THAN ROTATION.

ROTATION IS LAME.

STONEBACK IS STUPID.

HOW DO YOU SPELL "CYCLOPTOPUS?"

BEEP! BEEP! BEEP! I AM STONEBACK!

I BET ZIZZELLA LIKED GLITTER!

OK. OK! THE SUN IS A GIANT BURNING EYE!

AND IT'S KICKED INTO THE SKY BY AN ANGRY BARBARIAN. WRITE THAT IN YOUR NOTEBOOKS!

WOW. LOOK AT ALL THESE HARD WORKERS. GREAT JOB, MISS GILLIAN.

LIKE THE BOOTS?

=PIK=
=PIK=
=PIK=

EDDY, GET THAT PENCIL OUT OF YOUR NOSE.

BUT IT'S MY CULTURE.

NO, IT'S NOT. IT'S JUST GROSS.

IN THE SCHOOL YARD...

HEY, SWORDBOY, WHERE DO YOU COME FROM?

I COME FROM SKULLBANIA!

SKULL-LAME-IA? NEVER HEARD OF IT. IT MUST BE LAME.

YOU MAKE NO SENSE.

YOU ARE NOTHING BUT PESKY VERMIN.

SHUT UP OR I'LL HIT YOU!

HA! *YOU* HIT *ME*? I'VE BEEN IN THE JAWS OF A VIPER-CAT, FELT THE SPIT OF A FLAME-BULL. I DO NOT FEAR YOU.

SHUT UP, OR I'LL DO IT!

YOU ARE WEAK. YOUR PUNCH WOULD BE THAT OF A TIRED BABY.

BABY? I'M A THIRD-GRADER!

I AM A THIRD GRADER TOO...WITH A SWORD.

83

AFTER DROOL WAS CUT UP AND THE PIECES SEPARATED, HIS HEAD WAS PLACED IN A GUARDED TEMPLE.

THE GUARDS BEGAN TO PLAY GAMES. DROOL'S FOLLOWERS SNUCK IN AND WERE ABLE TO STEAL THE HEAD...

...WITHOUT EVEN A BATTLE.

IT IS THE MOST SHAMEFUL MOMENT IN ALL OF HISTORY.

WELL, THAT'S NOT GOING TO HAPPEN HERE.

I CANNOT HELP YOU, BILL THE BEAST.

FORGET IT! ALL YOU CARE ABOUT IS THAT STUPID BIG TOE OF DROOL!

WELL, IF THAT'S WHAT FANGBONE THINKS, THAT'S WHAT I THINK.

BILL! YOU ARE NOT A LOSER. YOU ARE A WARRIOR, AND A FRIEND.

BUT YOU SAID YOU CAN'T PLAY.

YOU HAVE WATCHED MY BACK, NOW I WILL WATCH YOURS. I WILL FIGHT WITH YOU! WE WILL DESTROY OUR ENEMIES. THE CHILDREN OF THEIR CHILDREN WILL FEAR US!

WHOA. WE JUST WANT TO WIN.

IF WE LOSE, ARE WE LEFT IN THE PIT OF SHAME WITH A TWO-TAILED SCORPION?

NO. WE GET A JUICE BOX.

TWEET!

ALL RIGHT! ARE THE TEAMS READY? YOU KNOW THE RULES! IF YOU GET HIT, YOU'RE OUT, AND THE FIRST TEAM WITH NO PLAYERS LEFT LOSES. IF YOU CATCH THE BALL, THE THROWER IS OUT. AND NO THROWING AT THE FACE!

BIP! BAM!

BAM! POW!

WINNER, AND CHAMPIONS! EXTREME ATTACK UNICORNS!

BILL! THE TOE IS WIGGLING MORE THAN EVER! A GREAT EVIL IS CLOSE!

WE HAVE BEATEN MONSTERS TWICE. THIS NEXT MONSTER WILL BE THE STRONGEST YET.

98

105

108

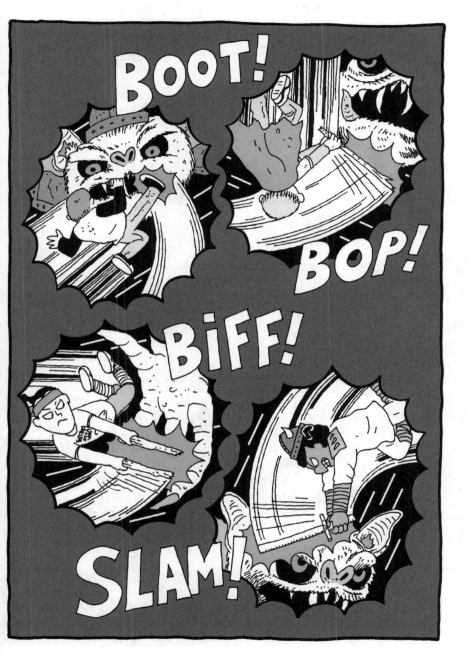

MY CLAN AND I OWE YOU A LIFE DEBT.

WITH YOU AT MY SIDE, WE CAN PROTECT THE BIG TOE OF DROOL FROM ANY VILE, HORRIBLE, WICKED, FOUL BEAST THAT VENOMOUS DROOL CAN THROW AT US! BE IT A TIGER-DRAGON, GORILLA-TROLL, OR LAVA-FERRET! WE SHALL FIGHT TO DEFEND THE HONORABLE CLANS OF SKULLBANIA! NO MATTER IF WE ARE EATEN, CRUSHED, TORTURED, OR PULLED LIMB FROM LIMB, WE WILL FIGHT! **FIGHT! FIGHT!**

OK...BUT WE HAVE A QUIZ FIRST.

QUIZ? WHAT IS QUIZ?

MICHAEL REX IS THE AUTHOR AND ILLUSTRATOR OF OVER 20 BOOKS FOR CHILDREN, INCLUDING *THE NEW YORK TIMES* #1 BESTSELLER, *GOODNIGHT GOON*. MICHAEL HAS A MASTER'S DEGREE IN VISUAL ARTS EDUCATION (K-12), AND WORKED AS A NYC ART TEACHER FOR FOUR YEARS. HE VISITS SCHOOLS ACROSS THE COUNTRY, AND HAS APPEARED ON "THE CELEBRITY APPRENTICE" AS A GUEST ILLUSTRATOR.

MIKE LIVES IN THE BRONX WITH HIS WIFE AND THEIR TWO BOYS.